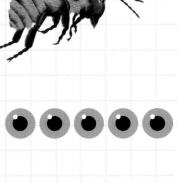

ANIMAL FACTS

BY THE NUMBERS

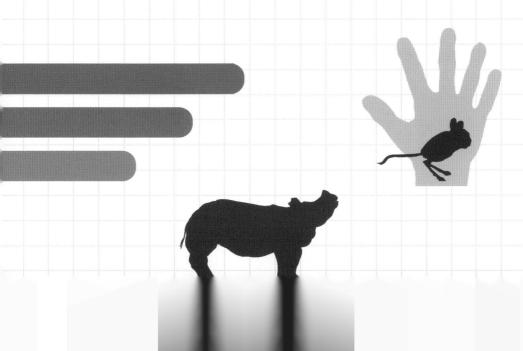

Contents

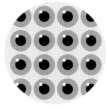

Animals live almost everywhere on earth. They can be found in scorching deserts and on polar ice caps. They survive on the tallest mountaintops and in the deepest parts of the sea. To exist in these different environments, animals have evolved an impressive range of shapes, sizes, and abilities.

These creatures include a rainforest frog the size of a blueberry and a whale as long as three school buses. There is a fly with a life span of just a few hours and a clam that can live for more than 500 years. And there is a fish that can swim as fast as a cheetah runs and a bat that sleeps for 20 hours a day.

Infographics — charts, graphs, diagrams, and illustrations — present information visually. The infographics in this book can help us appreciate some of the amazing creatures that share our world.

* Words in blue can be found in the glossary on page 38.

One million plus

Scientists have named about 1,400,000 different animal species. Most of them are insects. There are probably millions more species yet to be discovered.

spiders, mites, and scorpions
102,500 species

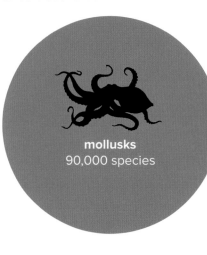

mollusks
90,000 species

other invertebrates
72,000 species

crustaceans
67,000 species

fish
33,000 species

birds
10,400 species

reptiles
10,000 species

amphibians
7,500 species

mammals
5,500 species

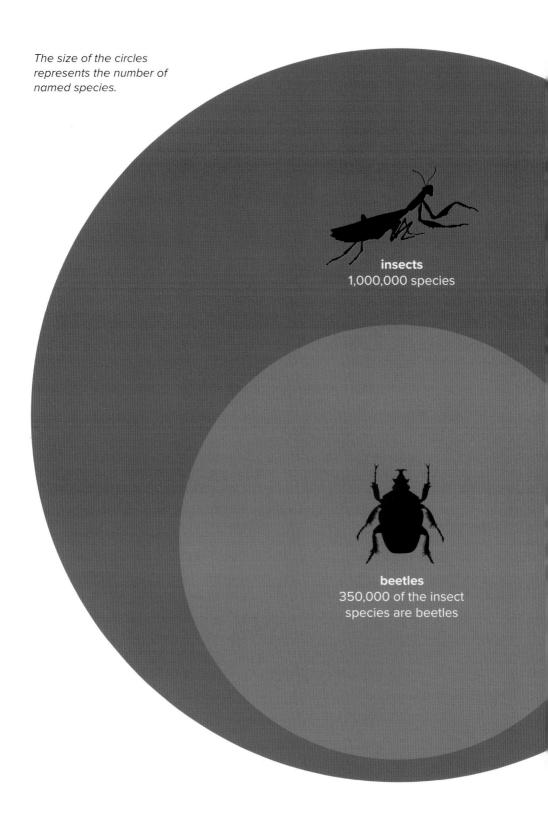

The size of the circles represents the number of named species.

insects
1,000,000 species

beetles
350,000 of the insect
species are beetles

How big?

These animals — some living, some extinct — are shown at the same scale (and compared to an adult human).

hippopotamus

wolf

manatee

Galápagos tortoise

Quetzalcoatlus

Siberian tiger

gorilla

oarfish

camel

Tyrannosaurus rex

great white shark

tuna

extinct animals

living animals

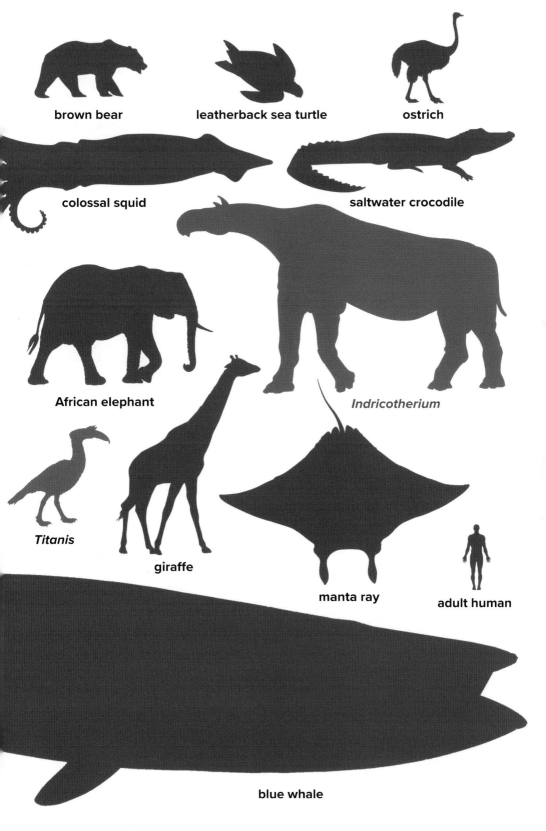

brown bear

leatherback sea turtle

ostrich

colossal squid

saltwater crocodile

African elephant

Indricotherium

Titanis

giraffe

manta ray

adult human

blue whale

How small?

These animals are shown life-size. Many of them are the smallest of their kind.

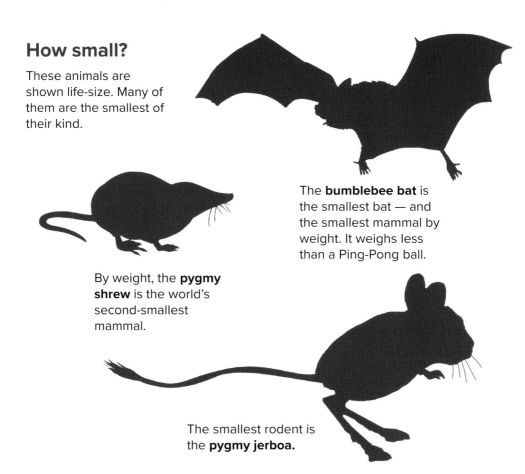

The **bumblebee bat** is the smallest bat — and the smallest mammal by weight. It weighs less than a Ping-Pong ball.

By weight, the **pygmy shrew** is the world's second-smallest mammal.

The smallest rodent is the **pygmy jerboa.**

Big and little

The pygmy jerboa compared to the world's largest rodent and an adult human's hand

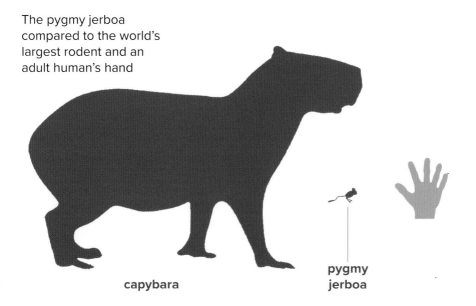

capybara

pygmy jerboa

The **bee hummingbird** is the smallest bird. It is not much larger than a bumblebee.

The **slender thread snake** is the smallest known species of snake.

The tiny **Amau frog** was discovered in 2012. By length, it is the world's smallest vertebrate.

A species of dwarf minnow is the world's smallest fish. It was considered the smallest vertebrate until the discovery of the Amau frog.

The smallest known spider is the *Patu digua*. It is shown above (inside the circle) at actual size, and greatly enlarged, below.

The Amau frog compared to the world's largest frog and an adult human's hand

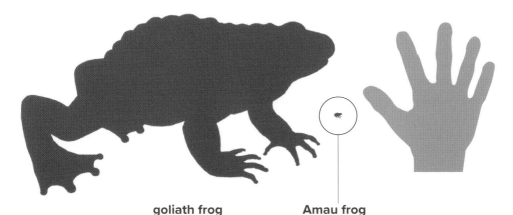

goliath frog   **Amau frog**

Speedy

The top speed of some of the fastest flying, running, and swimming animals — and a human

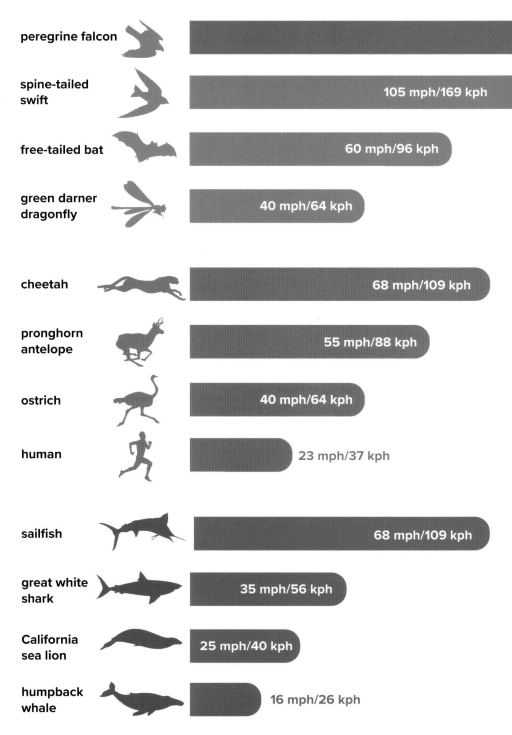

peregrine falcon

spine-tailed swift — 105 mph/169 kph

free-tailed bat — 60 mph/96 kph

green darner dragonfly — 40 mph/64 kph

cheetah — 68 mph/109 kph

pronghorn antelope — 55 mph/88 kph

ostrich — 40 mph/64 kph

human — 23 mph/37 kph

sailfish — 68 mph/109 kph

great white shark — 35 mph/56 kph

California sea lion — 25 mph/40 kph

humpback whale — 16 mph/26 kph

200 mph/322 kph

How many body lengths can an animal run in a second? The champion is a mite that is about the size of a sesame seed. (The fastest human can run slightly more than six body lengths per second.)

The sailfish, the fastest animal in water, is as fast as a cheetah. At top speed, it can swim ten body lengths per second.

Body lengths per second

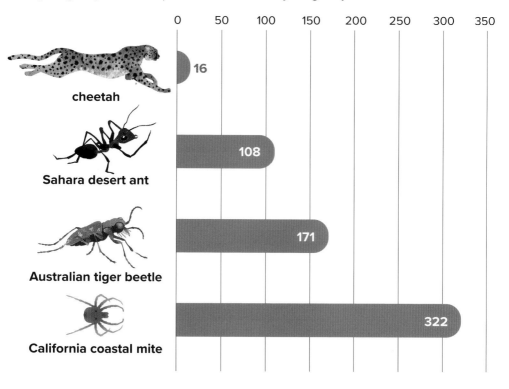

| | 0 | 50 | 100 | 150 | 200 | 250 | 300 | 350 |

cheetah — 16

Sahara desert ant — 108

Australian tiger beetle — 171

California coastal mite — 322

Sleepy

Almost all vertebrates sleep. And it's possible that other animals, such as insects and jellyfish, have periods of rest that are similar to sleep. But the amount of sleep that animals need varies greatly.

The **sloth** sleeps while hanging upside down. The sloth's claws can grip a branch even when it is sound asleep.

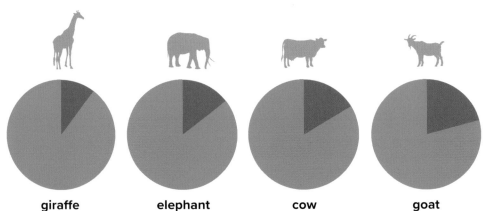

giraffe	elephant	cow	goat
2¹/₂ hours	3¹/₂ hours	4 hours	5 hours

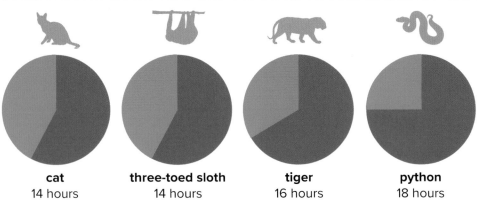

cat	three-toed sloth	tiger	python
14 hours	14 hours	16 hours	18 hours

● awake

● asleep

By wedging itself in the fork of a tree, a **koala** can sleep without falling.

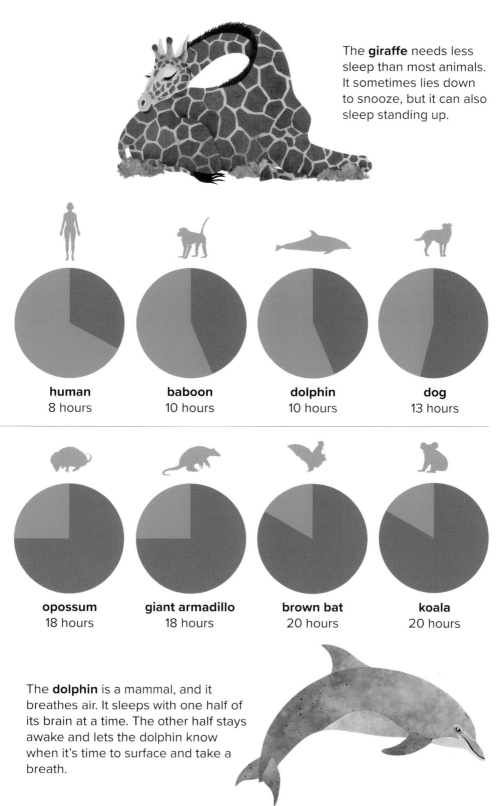

The **giraffe** needs less sleep than most animals. It sometimes lies down to snooze, but it can also sleep standing up.

human
8 hours

baboon
10 hours

dolphin
10 hours

dog
13 hours

opossum
18 hours

giant armadillo
18 hours

brown bat
20 hours

koala
20 hours

The **dolphin** is a mammal, and it breathes air. It sleeps with one half of its brain at a time. The other half stays awake and lets the dolphin know when it's time to surface and take a breath.

Fast and slow

Animal heartbeats vary from rapid whirs to slow thumps. The heart of a small animal beats more rapidly than that of a large creature.

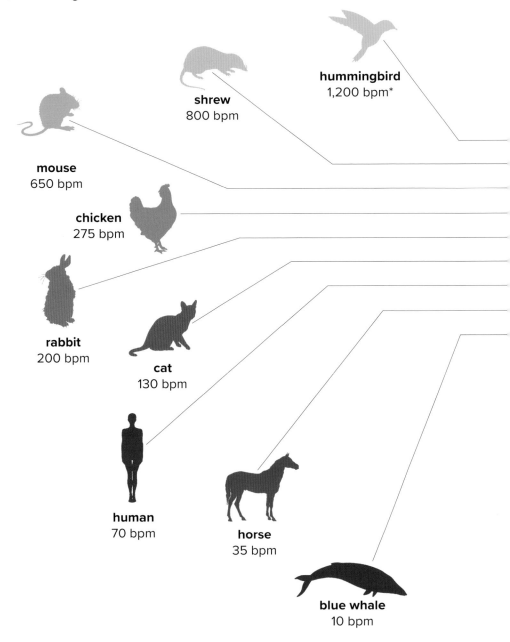

hummingbird
1,200 bpm*

shrew
800 bpm

mouse
650 bpm

chicken
275 bpm

rabbit
200 bpm

cat
130 bpm

human
70 bpm

horse
35 bpm

blue whale
10 bpm

bpm = beats per minute

hummingbird heart
(actual size)

blue whale heart
(compared to an adult
human)

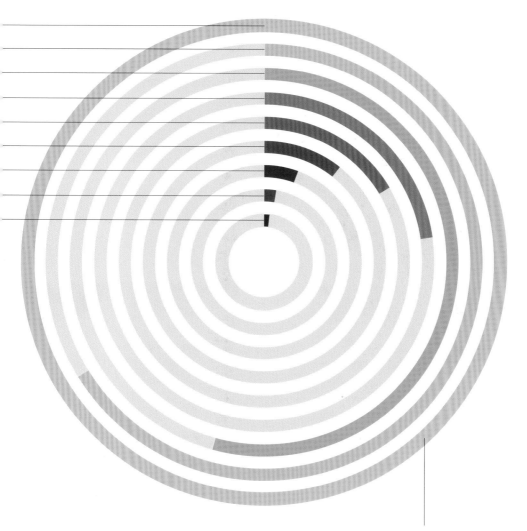

*complete circle = 1,200
beats per minute*

How many eyes?

Humans have two eyes. So do birds, other mammals, and many other creatures. But there are animals with many more eyes — and even an animal with a single eye.

This tiny creature's single eye is a light-sensitive spot, not an eye that can form clear images.

Like almost all vertebrates, this cat has two eyes.

This lizard has a third eye on the top of its head that can detect light.

This fish can look up and down at the same time.

Two of this insect's eyes form images, while three others detect light.

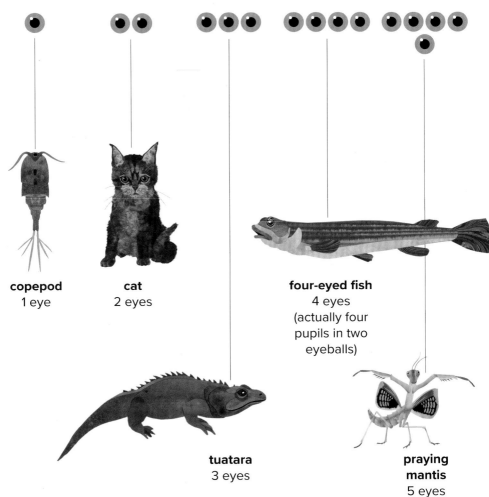

copepod
1 eye

cat
2 eyes

four-eyed fish
4 eyes
(actually four pupils in two eyeballs)

tuatara
3 eyes

praying mantis
5 eyes

A **scallop** can have as many as 200 eyes.

This spider's two big eyes see detail — the other six detect motion.

Two compound eyes form images. The crab's other eyes are light detectors.

In addition to two main eyes, there are five other crude eyes on each side of the scorpion's body.

The **sun star** has a simple eye at the tip of each of its arms.

This jellyfish's 24 eyes are arranged around its bell, or body.

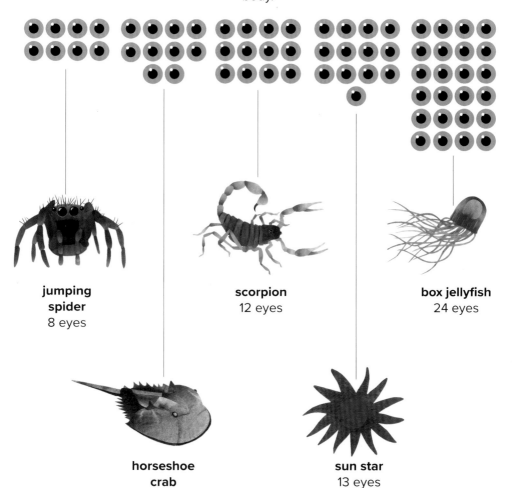

jumping spider
8 eyes

scorpion
12 eyes

box jellyfish
24 eyes

horseshoe crab
10 eyes

sun star
13 eyes

Life spans

Large animals usually live longer than small animals.

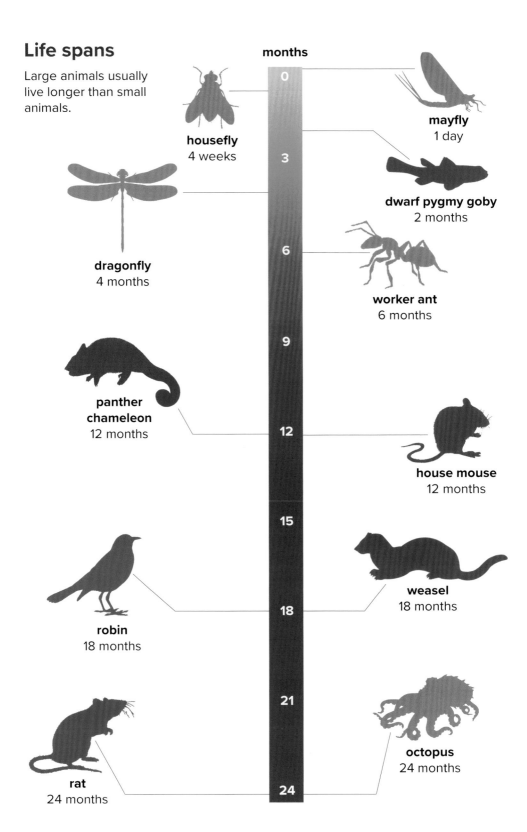

months

housefly
4 weeks

mayfly
1 day

dragonfly
4 months

dwarf pygmy goby
2 months

worker ant
6 months

panther chameleon
12 months

house mouse
12 months

robin
18 months

weasel
18 months

rat
24 months

octopus
24 months

0

3

6

9

12

15

18

21

24

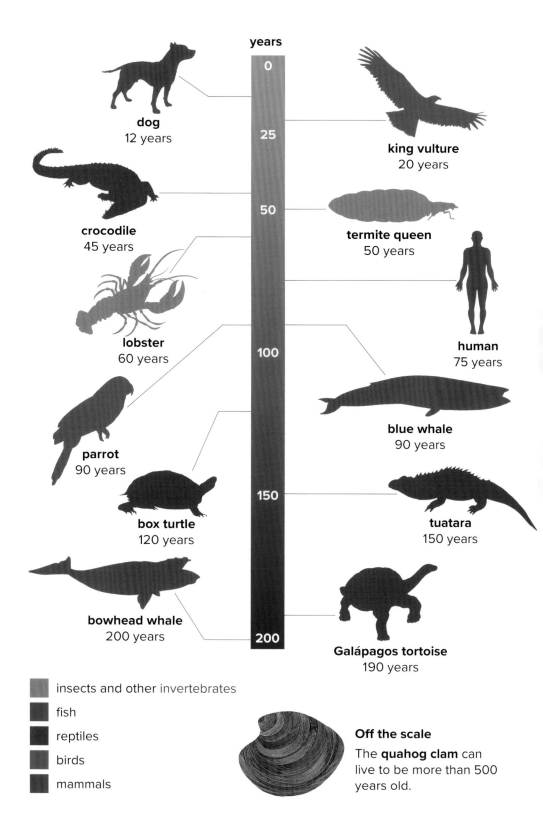

years

0

dog
12 years

king vulture
20 years

25

crocodile
45 years

50

termite queen
50 years

lobster
60 years

human
75 years

100

parrot
90 years

blue whale
90 years

box turtle
120 years

150

tuatara
150 years

bowhead whale
200 years

200

Galápagos tortoise
190 years

insects and other invertebrates
fish
reptiles
birds
mammals

Off the scale
The **quahog clam** can live to be more than 500 years old.

Noisy creatures

Some animals — even very small ones — can make surprisingly loud sounds. They may be signaling a mate, or saying "this is my territory."

By rubbing its legs together, the **bush cricket** makes a sound as loud as a chain saw.

The **coquí frog** gets its name from its ear-shattering call, which sounds like "CO–KEE."

hyena
110 decibels

bush cricket
110 decibels

macaw
105 decibels

alligator
90 decibels

coquí frog
100 decibels

90 DECIBELS   **100**   **110**

hair dryer

lawn mower

chain saw

The decibel is a unit used to measure the intensity of sound.

The call of the **bulldog bat** is one of the loudest sounds in the animal world. But it is so high-pitched that humans can't hear it.

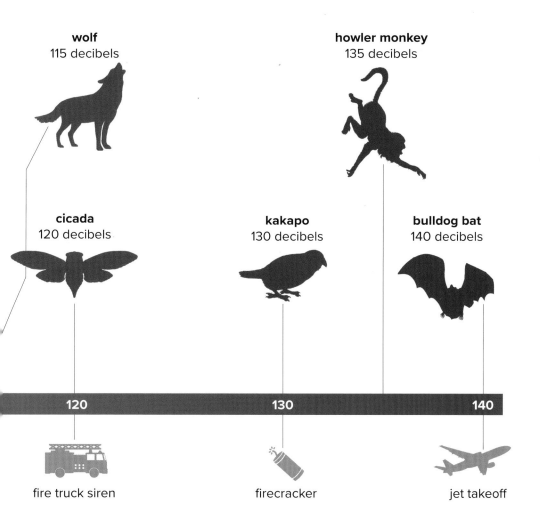

wolf
115 decibels

howler monkey
135 decibels

cicada
120 decibels

kakapo
130 decibels

bulldog bat
140 decibels

120   130   140

fire truck siren

firecracker

jet takeoff

The deadliest

The animals that cause the most human deaths are not always the ones that people are most afraid of.

Some 200 people a year die from an allergic reaction after being stung by a **bee**.

About 500 people each year are killed by the fiercely territorial **hippopotamus**.

The **crocodile** is the deadliest large animal. It kills an estimated 1,500 people a year.

Many people are terrified of **sharks**, but they kill only about 10 people a year.

Here are four of the world's most deadly animals:

fat-tailed scorpion
5,000 deaths — venomous sting

= 2,000 deaths per year

tsetse fly
10,000 deaths — carries disease

dog
55,000 deaths — about 500 from injury; most from disease transmitted by bites

snake
100,000 deaths — venomous bite

The **mosquito** is the deadliest of all. It can transmit several serious diseases, which kill an estimated one million people every year.

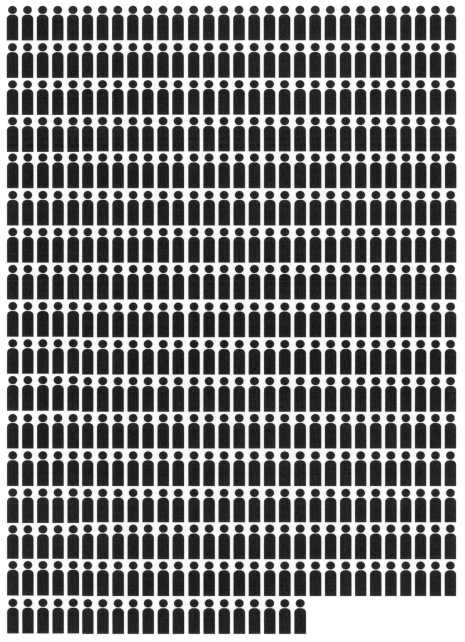

Venomous

Venomous animals inject their toxins with jaws, fangs, spines, stingers, or special stinging cells.

The **platypus** is one of the few venomous mammals. The male platypus has a spur on its back legs that can deliver a painful jab.

funnel-web spider
One of the world's two most venomous spiders (the Brazilian wandering spider is the other)

venom delivery: bite

box jellyfish
The most lethal jellyfish

venom delivery: stinging cells on tentacles

inland taipan
Though this snake is the world's most venomous, it is shy and unaggressive and causes few human deaths.

venom delivery: fangs

fat-tailed scorpion
Its venom is one of the strongest in the animal world.

venom delivery: stinger on tail

A person stung by a **box jellyfish** can die in as few as three minutes.

The circles represent the amount of toxin that will cause death. The smaller the circle, the more potent the venom or poison.

Poisonous

Poisonous animals have toxins in their skin, fur, feathers, or flesh. They must be touched or eaten for their poison to be dangerous.

The **Asian tiger snake** is the only snake that is both poisonous and venomous. It has poison glands on its neck, and it can also inject venom with its fangs.

puffer fish
This fish is eaten in Japan, where chefs must have a special license to serve it safely.

poison: in the flesh

cane toad
Predators that try to eat this toad often pay for this mistake with their life.

poison: squirts from a pair of glands on its neck

hooded pitohui
This bird gets its poison from the insects it feeds on.

poison: in the feathers and flesh

golden poison dart frog
This little frog has the most potent toxin in the animal world. One little frog contains enough poison to kill ten adult humans.

poison: in the skin

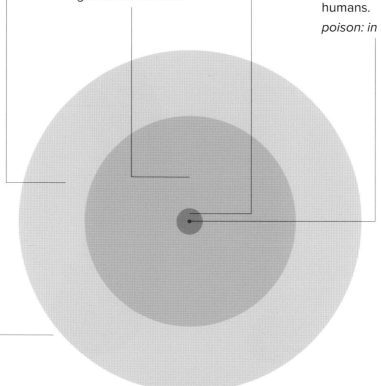

Bite and fight

Animal teeth — including fangs and tusks — come in different shapes and sizes. Animals use them for eating, fighting, injecting venom, and digging up plants.

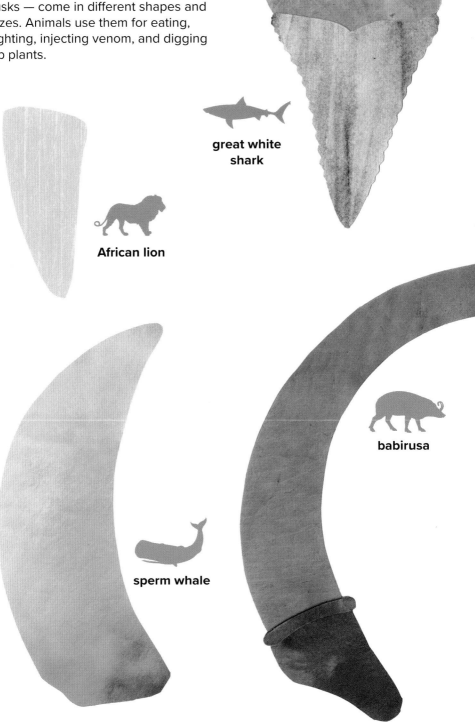

great white shark

African lion

babirusa

sperm whale

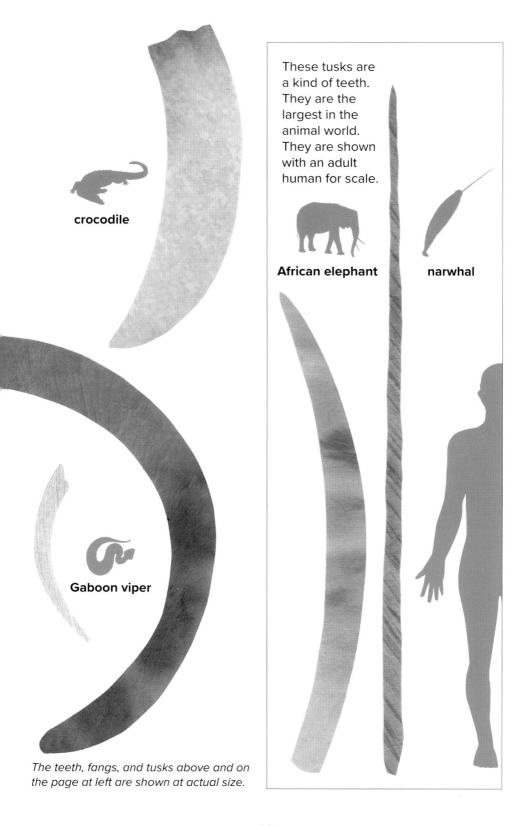

crocodile

These tusks are a kind of teeth. They are the largest in the animal world. They are shown with an adult human for scale.

African elephant

narwhal

Gaboon viper

The teeth, fangs, and tusks above and on the page at left are shown at actual size.

How life begins

A few fish, reptiles, and amphibians give birth to live young. And all mammals, except for the echidna and the platypus, have live babies. But most animals lay eggs. Some creatures lay just one egg at a time. Others produce thousands.

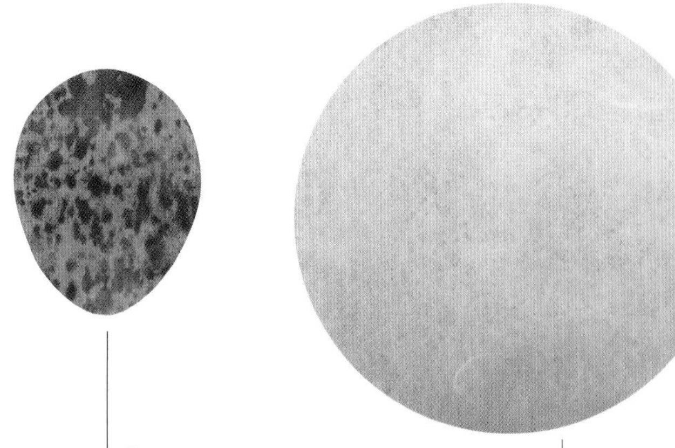

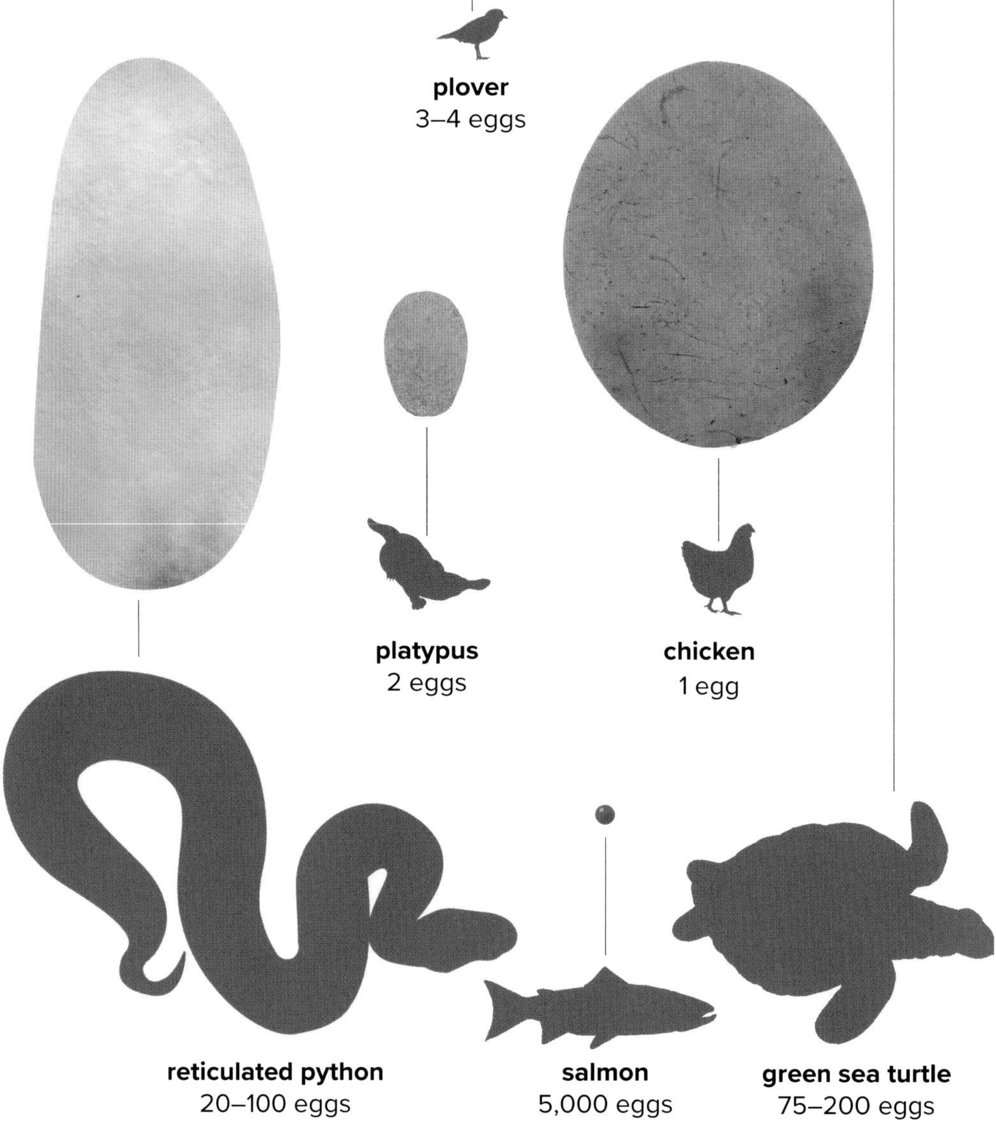

plover
3–4 eggs

platypus
2 eggs

chicken
1 egg

reticulated python
20–100 eggs

salmon
5,000 eggs

green sea turtle
75–200 eggs

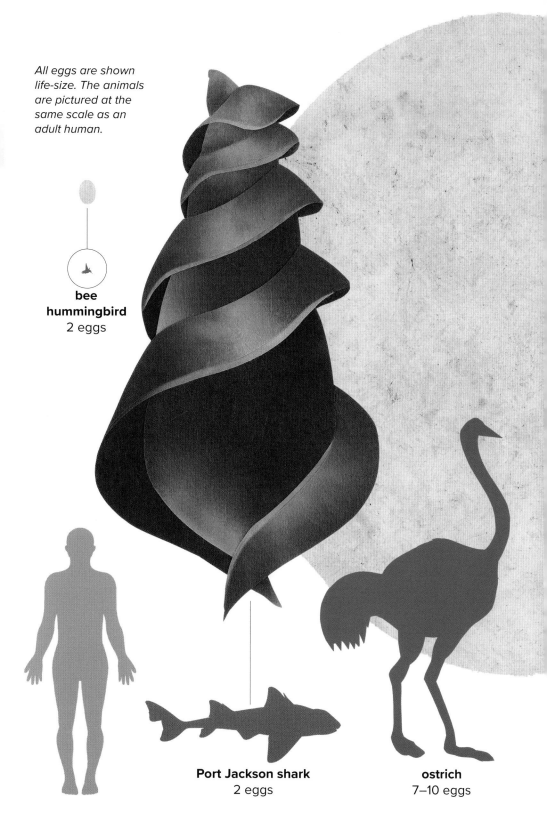

All eggs are shown life-size. The animals are pictured at the same scale as an adult human.

bee hummingbird
2 eggs

Port Jackson shark
2 eggs

ostrich
7–10 eggs

Big babies, little babies

It's not surprising that many large animals give birth to big babies. The biggest of all, a newborn blue whale, can weigh as much as three tons (2,722 kilograms). But other giant animals have small babies.

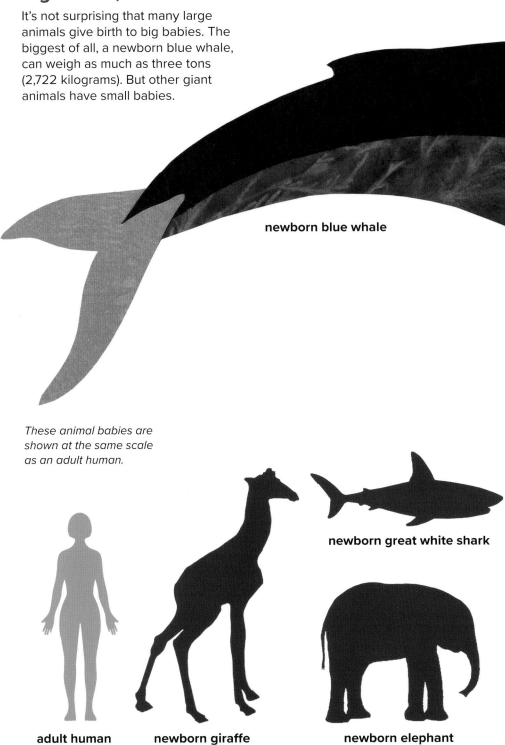

newborn blue whale

These animal babies are shown at the same scale as an adult human.

newborn great white shark

adult human

newborn giraffe

newborn elephant

These big creatures — shown below
at the same scale as an adult human
— produce tiny offspring. Their babies
are shown life-size.

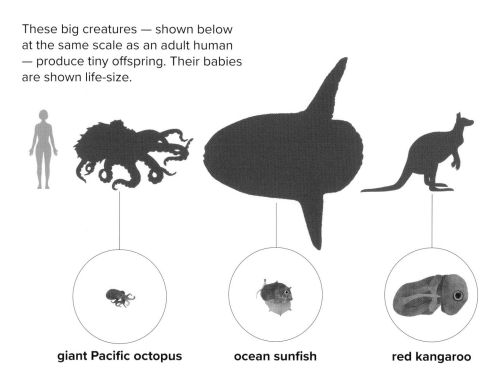

giant Pacific octopus   **ocean sunfish**   **red kangaroo**

After the dinosaurs

After the dinosaurs died out 66 million years ago, other giant creatures roamed the earth. These animals are all extinct now.

Megalodon was three times as long as a large great white shark (extinct 2¹/₂ million years ago).

Titanoboa was much larger than any snake alive today (extinct 58 million years ago).

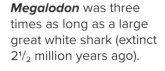

The **giant teratorn** was the largest bird that has ever flown (extinct six million years ago).

This giant **rat** lived in South America (extinct two million years ago).

The animals on this page are all shown at the same scale as this adult human.

Elasmotherium (e-**las**-mo-**there**-e-um) was a rhinoceros the size of an elephant (extinct 50,000 years ago).

The **giant ground sloth** was one of the largest land animals of its time. (extinct 12,000 years ago).

Kelenken, a species of terror bird, died out about 15 million years ago.

Daeodon, sometimes called the killer pig, was a fierce predator (extinct 18 million years ago).

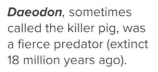

Animals in danger

Thousand of animal species around the world are in serious danger. Habitat loss, climate change, hunting, poaching, and overfishing are driving many animals to the edge of extinction.

The estimated number of individuals left in the wild, and where they live

gharial
650
Southeast Asia

North Atlantic right whale
400
Atlantic Ocean

kakapo
200
New Zealand

Assam rabbit
110
Southeast Asia

Amur leopard
80
China, Russia

Javan rhinoceros
60
Indonesia

Lord Howe Island stick insect
24
Lord Howe Island
(Australia)

vaquita
10
Gulf of California
(Mexico)

harlequin frog
4
Ecuador

Saharan addax
3
North Africa

Yangtze giant softshell turtle
3
China

Glossary

allergic reaction
The body's response to certain foreign substances. Sometimes the body's immune system overreacts, which can be harmful.

climate change
The gradual increase in global temperatures, changes in patterns of precipitation, and sea level rise. These changes are mostly caused by humans burning coal, oil, and other fossil fuels.

compound eyes
Eyes with many individual segments, each of which forms part of an image. They are found in insects and other arthropods.

decibel
A unit used to describe the intensity of sound. A ten decibel increase produces a sound that is ten times more intense.

echidna
Also known as a spiny anteater, the echidna, along with the platypus, is one of the two egg-laying mammals. It lives in Australia.

evolved
Changes in an animal's form or abilities that developed over many generations in response to changes in habitat, climate, or interactions with other animals.

extinct
No longer living. The term is applied to a particular species or group of organisms, not an individual.

habitat loss
The destruction of the places animals live. Habitat can be lost due to natural causes, such as a hurricane or wildfire. Often it's due to human activity such as clearing forests for farms or cities.

Indricotherium
An extinct relative of the modern rhinoceros. It lived about 20 million years ago in Asia, and was the largest mammal to ever live on land. It stood 18 feet (5½ meters) tall and weighed as much as five African elephants.

invertebrates
Animals without a backbone, including insects, worms, jellyfish, and many other creatures.

light-sensitive spot
A patch of light-sensitive cells on an animal that can detect light but not form an image.

poaching
Illegal hunting. Animals may be shot, trapped, or poisoned for food, trophies, or body parts that are sold illegally.

simple eye
An eye with a single lens. More complex than a light-sensitive spot, but not capable of forming images.

species
Members of the same animal species usually look alike, act alike, and can mate and produce offspring.

stinging cells
Specialized cells found in jellyfish, anemones, and other animals. These cells contain a hair-like trigger that fires a venomous barb when touched.

territorial
An animal that defends its territory, usually against others of the same species but sometimes against any animal that it sees as a trespasser.

terror bird
Flightless, meat-eating birds that lived in the Americas from 60 million to about 2 million years ago. They were fast runners with big, sharp beaks. *Kelenken,* the largest of these birds, was one of the top predators of its time.

toxin
A poison or venom produced by a living organism.

vertebrate
An animal with a backbone. Fish, reptiles, amphibians, birds, and mammals are all vertebrates.

Bibliography

Amazing Animals Q&A. By David Burnie. DK Publishing, 2007.

Amazing Numbers in Biology. By Rainer Flindt. Springer, 1996.

The Animal Book. By Steve Jenkins. Houghton Mifflin Harcourt, 2013.

Animal Fact File. By Dr. Tony Hare. Checkmark Books, 1999.

Animal Records. By Mark Carwardine. Sterling, 2008.

Egg: Nature's Perfect Package. By Steve Jenkins and Robin Page. Houghton Mifflin Harcourt, 2015.

The Encyclopedia of Animals. Edited by Dr. Per Christiansen. Amber Books, 2006.

Life. By Martha Holmes and Michael Gunton. University of California Press, 2010.

The Life of Mammals. By David Attenborough. Princeton University Press, 2002.

Nature's Predators. By Michael Bright, Robin Kerrod, and Barbara Taylor. Hermes House, 2002.

Sleep and Rest in Animals. By Corine Lacrampe. Firefly Books, 2003.

Venom, Poison, and Electricity. By Kimberley Jane Pryor. Marshall Cavendish, 2010.

Weird, Wild, Amazing! By Tim Flannery. Norton Young Readers, 2019.

Wildlife Factfinder. By Martin Walters. Dempsey Parr, 1999.

The World of Animals. By Desmond Morris. Jonathan Cape, 1993.

For Henry

Clarion Books is an imprint of HarperCollins Publishers.

Animal Facts by the Numbers
Copyright © 2022 by Steve Jenkins

clarionbooks.com

ISBN: 978-0-358-47012-0 hardcover
ISBN: 978-0-358-47013-7 paperback

The illustrations are cut- and torn-paper collage.
The infographics are cut-paper silhouettes and the graphics are created digitally.
The text type was set in Proxima Nova.
The display type was set in Berthold Akzidenz Grotesk.

Manufactured in Italy
ROTO 10 9 8 7 6 5 4 3 2 1
4500846446

First Edition